A PERFECT COUPLE
Or:
Let Your Heart Break Open

Brooke Berman

G000067469

BROADWAY PLAY PUBLISHING INC
224 E 62nd St, NY, NY 10065
www.broadwayplaypub.com
info@broadwayplaypub.com

A PERFECT COUPLE
© Copyright 2008 by Brooke Berman

First printing: December 2008
Second printing: June 2010
I S B N: 978-0-88145-426-0

Book design: Marie Donovan
Word processing: Microsoft Word
Typographic controls: Ventura Publisher & Adobe InDesign
Typeface: Palatino
Printed and bound in the U S A

A PERFECT COUPLE was commissioned by Arielle Tepper Productions.

A PERFECT COUPLE was developed at The National Theatre in London, Naked Angels, New Dramatists, and in WET's INKubator: The Ray and Kit Sawyer Development Series.

The world premiere of A PERFECT COUPLE was produced by WET Productions (Women's Expressive Theater, Inc, Sasha Eden and Victoria Pettibone, Producers) at the DR2 Theater in New York City, opening on 18 June 2008. The cast and creative contributors were:

EMMA.. Annie McNamara
ISAAC ....James Waterston
AMY ....Dana Eskelson
JOSH ....Elan Moss-Bachrach

Director...Maria Mileaf
Set design .... Neil Patel
Costume design.. Jenny Mannis
Lighting design .... Matthew Richards
Sound design.. Bart Fasbender
Casting director .... Alaine Alldaffer
Press representative ....Spin Cycle/Ron Lasko
Production manager ....Ralph Carhart
Production stage manager ....Larry K Ash
Associate producers ....Ami Ankin & Azizah Rowen

CHARACTERS & SETTING

ISAAC, *forty, about to be married*

AMY, *thirty-nine, about to be married*

EMMA, *thirty-nine, their single best friend. Or best single friend. Or both.*

JOSH, *twenty-three, a recent college grad, lives with his parents, nearby*

Place: an old family house in the country. Ghosts.

NOTE

Stylistically this moves from traditional "scenes" to "arias" and "duets", in which characters speak directly to the audience, sometimes on their own, sometimes in choral relief with other characters and then, back to scene. The arias are straightforward, simply presented—presentational rather than introspective or psychological—like documentary. Or the breakout sections of reality T V shows. Or opera. The characters love talking to the audience. And to one another. They are effusive beings.

The overall tone of this play should be quick, rigorous, playful and smart.

The original title was "Let Your Heart Break Open" because in my experience, once your heart actually breaks apart, it can take on new life, new light— heartbreak is a triumph. The world can now enter! Thus, the loss of a relationship is not necessarily a sad topic. There is liberation in sight, and deeper relationship with both self and other.

To achieve the intended tone, it will help for the actors to make big positive choices with their text and actions—until the journal appears and everyone discovers that they know just a little less about themselves than they'd imagined. The shifts in tone and subject matter occur in spite of themselves, taking us by surprise.

THANKS

Seth Glewen, Arielle Tepper Madover, The Royal National Theatre Studo and Orla O'Loughlin, Rachel Neuberger, Bill Haber, Michael Cardonick, Olivier Sultan, Denyce Mylson, Francine Volpe and the lovely ladies of WET, Penney Leyshon, and Gordon Haber.

scene:
a perfect couple

(*Early morning.* EMMA, *in the kitchen alone. She makes a pot of coffee though a cone-shaped device, enjoying the absence of electric coffee makers. She scoops coffee into the cone, waiting for the water to boil.* EMMA *seems to know where things are in this kitchen, moving through the room with a great deal of ease, even though it is not hers.* EMMA *snoops a little. Looks in every drawer. Just to see what's there. She's happy in a strange quiet way. Everyone else, asleep. She is at home in this kitchen, comfortable. The water boils.* EMMA *pours it through the cone-shaped device and lets the coffee brew. Impatiently. She opens the refrigerator and sees berries. Starts to wash and cut strawberries, popping one into her mouth as she does this. All of this is quiet, familiar—*)

(ISAAC *enters. A sweet ease between them*)

EMMA: You can't go into the world and find Love the way you find a pair of shoes.

ISAAC: What?

EMMA: I'm just saying.

(ISAAC *looks at* EMMA *a moment.*)

ISAAC: I need coffee. (*He goes to it, pours himself a cup. Then,*) You can't go into the world and what?

EMMA: Find love the way you find a pair of shoes.

ISAAC: Some people do it just like that.

EMMA: Not me.

ISAAC: Which is exactly why we love you. Everything has to be hard.

EMMA: Not hard. Honest.

ISAAC: Idealized.

EMMA: Enough.

(ISAAC *comes to* EMMA, *sits. Eats a strawberry. Starts to cut fruit as well, dismembering a pineapple. A sweet ease between them.*)

EMMA: I've been thinking about Coral all morning. How we sat here, talking, she said— *(She cuts herself suddenly. Blood)* Shit. *(She puts her finger in her mouth.)*

ISAAC: Come here.

(ISAAC *puts* EMMA's *finger under a stream of water.*)

EMMA: Fucking—shit!

ISAAC: It's okay. Here.

(ISAAC *gets a band-aid, takes* EMMA's *finger out of the water, dries it on his shirt, and then wraps the band-aid around it.*)

EMMA: Why are you doing this? Now?

ISAAC: Taking care of your finger?

EMMA: No. Not that. Why are you—? You know.

ISAAC: It's the right time.

EMMA: But are you—?

ISAAC: Yes?

EMMA: —sure?

ISAAC: Yes. I'm sure.

EMMA: *(She is about to raise an objection, but decides not to.)* Okay.

ISAAC: Relationships take work.

EMMA: Okay.

ISAAC: And we have worked.

EMMA: I know.

ISAAC: Besides, it's a good time. We're ready. It's time.

EMMA: Okay. *(Beat)* But...

ISAAC: Yes?

EMMA: You don't get along.

ISAAC: Well.

EMMA: You can't be alone together.

ISAAC: That's not true.

EMMA: You run away from her. You're always traveling, and when you do come home, you fight. I love you both, but you make each other sick.

ISAAC: Well. That's what real relationships are like. You make each other sick. I think that's real.

EMMA: Really.

ISAAC: Really. There is this part of the adult long-term relationship where you learn to transcend the things you hate about the other person. Where you make each other sick, and stay anyway. This is commitment. This is real. You wouldn't know because you haven't had an actual relationship, with an actual adult in—

EMMA: That's not true.

ISAAC: —a long time.

EMMA: Not true!

ISAAC: Isn't it?

EMMA: No. Besides, I've been really busy.

ISAAC: I see.

EMMA: And you can't just—

ISAAC: I know. Go into the world and—

EMMA: That's right.

ISAAC: Amy and I know each other. We're committed. Dedicated. Intimate. At a certain point, you can't start over. And you can't run away. Everyone says so. And everyone says relationships take work.

EMMA: Is that what "Everyone" says?

ISAAC: We want this. We're forty. It's time.

EMMA: I'm still thirty-nine.

ISAAC: Well, I'm forty, and I will marry Amy.

(AMY *enters in a nice robe. Just waking up*)

AMY: God, I hope you'll marry me. I've already hired caterers.
  Oh, Coffee. (*Coffee should sound a little bit like Nirvana.*)

(AMY *heads for her favorite morning thing, touching the others lightly as she does. But really, she's all about the coffee, still adjusting to being awake. She does not do morning well. Then, sensing that she has walked into something—*)

AMY: What are you two doing?

ISAAC & EMMA: Nothing. Talking.

AMY: Oh. (*Then, looking out the window*) Do you think I'll be able to fit seventy-five guests on that lawn? I'm going to make that happen.

ISAAC: Emma wants to know why we're getting married.

EMMA: Why now?

AMY: Because we're grownups. Because people who have been together for fifteen years get married or break up and we're not breaking up. That is why.

(AMY *goes upstairs, kissing* ISAAC *as she goes. They watch after her.*)

ISAAC: The house looks good, right?

EMMA: It's great.

ISAAC: We've been fixing things. We have this kid next door; he's great—just graduated from school. Has time on his hands. Can use the cash. We're going to fix everything.

EMMA: Is there a lot to fix?

ISAAC: It's an old house. And since Coral died...

EMMA: It's just like it was. When you came downstairs just now, it was just like it was. Coral said, "The thing you want wants you back."

ISAAC: I don't understand.

EMMA: "The thing you want wants you back" You don't have to look for it because odds are, it is already very close. It is already yours.

ISAAC: I still don't understand.

EMMA: Well, it's a general life philosophy. You don't have to force things, or push them into— What don't you understand? *(Changing the subject)* I don't feel old enough to be our age. Do you?

ISAAC: Yes. More and more, I am starting to feel old enough to be Our Age.

EMMA: The marriage thing.

ISAAC: And for you, the lack of it.

EMMA: Lets bring Amy breakfast in bed. Strawberries. More coffee. She loves breakfast in bed. When we were roommates—

ISAAC: I know. You had breakfast in bed all the time.

EMMA: We did.

(Playfully, they assemble a plate to take to AMY *and perhaps the entire pot of coffee.* EMMA *exits, but* ISAAC *stops on his way upstairs, turning to the audience, for Aria #1:)*

aria #1:
a house in the country, with trains every hour

ISAAC: We got this place when I was a kid. It was a weekend house, at first. But Coral, my father's eccentric Swiss second wife, fell in love with this part of the country. It became her home in a way that our apartment in the City, where he'd lived with my mother, was not. This was entirely hers. Eventually, they moved up here full time. She was some kind of amateur everything. And she made friends like no one else I know. People loved Coral. She was my mother, even though she wasn't. And this was her house. And now it is mine.

Over the years, we have, I have, maybe half a dozen friends up here. Plus the people who remember Coral. Many people remember Coral. And my father. They threw parties. People remember them. People came to tea. People came over. This house was once—alive— in ways that it hasn't been since she died. I'd like it to be that way again. Alive. People say, well people say, the way to do that is to marry Amy and have some kids. That is what people say.

I don't know about kids. I never have. But Amy wants kids, Amy has always wanted kids, and Amy is usually right. About everything. Sometimes I think, what if I am very fucked up and what if Amy, maybe, is right?

(ISAAC exits after EMMA)

scene:
why do people love to talk about the past?

(JOSH *enters. Looks around. Calls for the owners of the house.*)

JOSH: Hello? Hey? Isaac? Amy?

(JOSH *pokes around, pours himself a cup of coffee. Checks out the stuff on the kitchen table. Looks for a note addressed to him, doesn't find it. Waits, until* AMY *enters*)

AMY: I thought I heard you. Want some//

JOSH: Is that okay? I just//

AMY: Oh you found it. Of course it's—

JOSH: Okay.

AMY: Our friend's up from the City. Have you ever met Emma?

(JOSH *shakes his head no*)

AMY: I didn't think so. She's my best friend. We went to school together. Lived together before I met— *(Motions upstairs, as if to signify* ISAAC*)* —Do you want food, Sweetheart? I know we have— *(Strawberries)*

JOSH: No I'm okay. Do you want me to...? We were going to work on—

AMY: The attic. I know. Isaac's kind of— we're getting a late start. We were all up pretty late. Talking about the past. Why do people love to talk about the past?

JOSH: I don't know.

AMY: There's this wish to recreate your history together by talking about it. Sometimes we don't know what to talk about besides that. So we talk about what we did and who we were. And it's all very entertaining. Except that it isn't, and it's a huge waste of time because we're not those people anymore. Do you know what I mean? You don't, do you?

JOSH: Sure. I mean, my friends do that too. Just on a smaller scale.

AMY: You do?

JOSH: Totally. Hey, I'm reading the book you gave me.

AMY: Do you like it?

JOSH: I like how it's put together. Events could happen in any order and it would be the same.

AMY: That's what I like too. I think it makes more sense. That's how we remember them anyway. I should give you—Isaac gave me this book I haven't been able to get through maybe you'd like it. It's a bunch of fragments, half history and half fiction, and you're not meant to know what's what. It annoys me.

JOSH: Annoys you how?

AMY: I like to know.

JOSH: Why?

AMY: I don't know. I just do. Don't you?

JOSH: I guess I don't care so much.

AMY: Everyone says it's brilliant, this book. Isaac loved it. It's just—

JOSH: What?

AMY: I like to know what's what.

JOSH: Do you guys need time?

AMY: In what sense?

JOSH: Uh, now. This morning. Do you want me to— I have to go into town. So, like, I could go do that and you know, give you guys some more—

AMY: That might be good.

JOSH: Can I get you anything? In town? I have to pay—
fucking parking tickets—and overdue book fines.
So, I'm going to the D M V and the library, and I could
totally swing by, you know, whatever you need—

AMY: Well. No, it's all right. I can go later.

JOSH: You sure? Because I have to go anyway, and it's
like—I'd love to save you a—

AMY: Well. Actually. Yes. I could use—just a few
groceries—if you have time.

JOSH: The Stop and Shop awaits. Super Stop and Shop.
The big one. The granddaddy Stop and Shop. El Mega
Grande Big Motherfucking—

AMY: Thank you. And you have to stay for dinner.
Will you stay? You'll love Emma.

JOSH: Yeah. I'll stay.

AMY: Good.

(AMY *writes a list for* JOSH. *He drinks more coffee. Watches
her. Looks around at stuff. She finishes and hands him the
list.*)

AMY: Thank you for doing this, Sweetheart.

JOSH: No problem. I'll be back—

AMY: I'll have Isaac ready.

JOSH: Right on.

(JOSH *goes.* AMY *watches him go.*)

AMY: Yes. Right on.

aria #2:
i will not be receiving you

EMMA: Hello, You.
This is a message.
For you.
Not an actual phone call.
Just a message.

I've missed your mind—
Your strange hungry sad inquisitive mind.
And all those nights we stayed up talking.
Do you miss me, I mean, mine?

I'm out of town.
Away with friends, my oldest friends
You can't call me here
My cell phone does not get reception.
Which means, I will not be receiving you.
So you can't call.

scene:
your great adventure

EMMA: Men are taught that the Grand Adventure of their lives will be work. Women are taught that it will be Relationship. We move through the world looking for our grand adventure in the form of romantic love, deep friendship, erotic connection. Men move through the world looking to create, to build, to fight. We look for people to connect with. And this, I think, is the problem. It's a difference in expectation.

ISAAC: That sounds right.

AMY: It doesn't sound right.

EMMA: *(To* AMY*) You* stopped working.

AMY: So? I don't *define* myself by work the way you two do. My job was my job. Yours are both—

EMMA: But that's my point. That's my point exactly.

AMY: It doesn't mean the wedding is the Grand Adventure of my life.

EMMA: You act like it is.

AMY: I do not. *(To* ISAAC*)* Honey, Josh was here. He came to help you work on—

ISAAC: Oh shit. The attic.

AMY: Right. So I sent him away—he's off getting groceries and paying his library book fines—but you have to be ready when he gets back. So. Go. Hurry. Leave me for the attic. You can be dressed by the time he—

ISAAC: Amy, you can't just send him to the store.

AMY: What do you mean?

ISAAC: Is he getting groceries for us?

AMY: He offered.

ISAAC: He's here to work on the house. He's not your personal assistant.

AMY: He's my friend, and he offered.

ISAAC: And he's going to bill me for his time because I pay him by the hour. To work on the house.

AMY: He offered. And he showed up ready to work and you were busy. And he'll be back in an hour, so, you should maybe get the attic ready. Or yourself.

(ISAAC *leaves, ostensibly to get ready for* JOSH *and the attic.*)

AMY: *(Calling after him)* And I invited him for dinner. So, will you cook? Please? *(And back to* EMMA*)* Isaac's become the most amazing cook. He cooks food from every place he's traveled. He can taste something once

and recreate it. The only good thing about how much
he travels is how it's improved our culinary lives.

EMMA: You have a whole world here.

AMY: Sometimes. Sometimes it's like that. *(Changing
the subject)* I want you to find someone.

EMMA: I'm kind of taking a break from all that.
"Finding Someone". I'd sort of just like to live my life,
you know?

AMY: I don't believe you.

EMMA: What don't you believe?

AMY: You used to want to get married.

EMMA: Sure. But that's not what happened. Marriage
didn't happen. To me. Yet. And I'm not even sure I
believe in—

AMY: Use your will. Make it happen.

EMMA: How?

AMY: Take action.

EMMA: You didn't meet Isaac that way.

AMY: But every single step of the way, I'm the one
who has made the relationship "happen". And it's all
working out. We are finally getting married. We have
dated, we have taken breaks, we have broken up, we
have seen other people, we have gotten back together,
we have been long distance, short distance, we live
together, we bought a condo, sold it, made a profit.
We went through: an abortion, a new business, two
of his fellowships, weddings of all of our friends
(except for you) —And who is the one who constantly
makes it okay to take each new step? Me. I am the one
who does this. I do this because I can do this. Because
I am not afraid. Because I had good parenting. I am the
one who knows it is permissible—no, pleasurable—
to take Next Steps. So. I am the one who laid the

ultimatum on the table, and Isaac responds really well to ultimatums. I give him structure. He needs that. He loves me for the structure I impose. Because otherwise, he'd be lost. You may think you know Isaac, but I can attest to the fact that without me, Isaac would be lost—
stranded—literally—in an airport somewhere, between flights, on a layover, lost. We meet each others' needs. I provide—

EMMA: An itinerary?

AMY: You can't wait for things to happen. Use your will. Find a partner so that you are not alone. Get practical. Realistic. Change the kind of men you date. Change your expectations. Change your whole way of doing things. In fact, I've heard, I've heard, people say, if you just start doing every single thing in a new way, you will get new results.

EMMA: Technically, I'm not "dating" them.

AMY: Look. I love you. I love you, and I want you to be happy like me.

EMMA: That's so funny. Because I want you to be happy like me.

AMY: You don't understand. You were never on the Baby Track.

EMMA: There was a "Baby Track"?

AMY: Yes. And you were not on it.

EMMA: Were you?

AMY: Women who don't have babies go insane.

EMMA: You're kidding.

AMY: There are statistics. Studies. It's true.

EMMA: Who conducted these studies?

AMY: My mother told me.

EMMA: Your mother?

AMY: She came across these studies.

EMMA: I don't have babies. And I'm not insane.
And your mother is—

AMY: Look at the statistics. We have to have babies.
Otherwise we feel some kind of essential loss.

EMMA: I don't feel essential loss!

AMY: What about the phone calls?

EMMA: What phone calls?

AMY: In the middle of the night. The ones that sound
like you're drowning. Every single time you get your
heart broken, you call, and you sound like you're
drowning. Like you are under water, and you can't
swim or breathe. And you think you can call any time
you want. Like that. When you can't swim or breathe.
And like I'm just supposed to—

EMMA: There weren't that many, there aren't that many
phone calls.

AMY: You get your heart broken a lot. And it's not your
fault. You don't know any better. I'm not blaming you.
I'm just saying. You get your heart broken a lot. And
you call. And I don't always know—

EMMA: You're my best friend.

AMY: But at a certain point, Em, you have to take
responsibility. You have to get on a better path.

EMMA: The Baby Track.

AMY: It's okay, Em. Isaac wasn't on that track either.
But now, we are all going to get on the same track.
Except you. I don't know what track you want to be
on. But Isaac and I are getting on the same track.

EMMA: (Incredulous) Are you having a baby?

AMY: It's on the table.

EMMA: What table?

AMY: The proverbial table. Babies are on the proverbial table. Isaac just needs time. (*Changing tracks, another scathingly brilliant idea*) You know, you should call Wendy.

EMMA: Wendy?

AMY: She's single.

EMMA: Is she?

AMY: Wendy meets guys all the time.

EMMA: I meet guys all the time.

AMY: Wendy meets guys online, or sometimes at Singles events, readings, bars even, and she really likes them. And Wendy is always looking for girls to go out with. I think it helps to meet men when you go out with your girlfriends. You don't look desperate. But you do look available. And if you sit in upscale bars, the kind where the drinks are expensive enough that you know the men have jobs. And you're much cuter than Wendy, so if she can meet—

EMMA: Amy. I'm not going to sit in upscale bars with Wendy trying to pick up men with jobs. It's just not about that.

AMY: What's it about then?

(JOSH *enters, with groceries from Stop & Shop. The following two lines may overlap quite a bit.*)

AMY: Because if I were single, I'd be sitting in upscale bars with Wendy.

JOSH: Hey. I'm back. I'll put the groceries on the—

AMY: I'll get Isaac.

(AMY *leaves.* EMMA/JOSH *alone.* JOSH, *like* EMMA, *moves around this kitchen as if it is his.*)

EMMA: I'm Emma.

JOSH: Hey.

EMMA: Hey.

(Beat)

JOSH: You're visiting from—?

EMMA: The City.

(Beat)

JOSH: So you guys have like, all been friends for a long time, huh?

EMMA: Yep. A long time. And you—

JOSH: —live next door. Well. My folks do. I'm kind of freeloading right now, so I kind of live next door, only it's temporary, so I don't like, *live*, there, at least that's what I tell myself about that.

EMMA: Did you know Coral?

JOSH: Totally. We used to hang out. When I was home from school. We'd kind of like—we played guitar and smoked pot. I mean, I did. She watched. And we had great talks. About every single part of life. We both just loved to talk. She told me things.

EMMA: What kind of things?

(ISAAC and AMY return.)

ISAAC: Josh, I'm yours

AMY: *(Turning to the task at hand)* Just bring whatever you think should come downstairs—down. And we can sort through it all down here. I want to make sure we get rid of anything skanky, donate anything donate-able, sell anything we want to sell, basically clean out and make room. *(To EMMA)* He's terrible at getting rid of—

ISAAC: We'll be fine.

(They start to go. AMY, calls after them.)

AMY: Okay. But make sure—Josh, make sure that you actually do find things we can get rid of— And also, if there's anything that needs repair. Or cleaning. We'll sort everything into piles once it's down here.

ISAAC: (*From offstage*) Amy. We're adults. We can figure this out.

AMY: Okay. Fine. Figure it out. (*Back to* EMMA) They won't throw anything away. He's terrible with—

EMMA: So why don't you do it?

AMY: He wanted to.

sequence:
figuring it out

(*Lights on* ISAAC *and* JOSH *in a part of the stage designated "attic". Quickly and without changes, well jump-cut to* AMY *and* EMMA *in the "kitchen".*)

ISAAC: Don't get married, Josh.

JOSH: Okay.

ISAAC: It looks good. But don't do it.

JOSH: Sure.

ISAAC: It's not what it's cracked up to be.

JOSH: I see.

ISAAC: Do you have a girlfriend?

JOSH: Not right now. I did. But not right now.

ISAAC: Don't marry her.

JOSH: Okay. I mean, I can't because, you know, we don't even talk right now. She's living in Amsterdam, she met this guy. He sounds nuts. He used to live as part of this underground free-love community where people...

ISAAC: I'm not saying, *no one* should do it. I'm not saying *I* shouldn't do it—

JOSH: Fucking trust-fund hippies.

ISAAC: I'm just saying—

JOSH: Sure.

ISAAC: You think all these things are true, or will be true, and only half of what you think is true *is*— and then, all these other things come into play— and then, somewhere along the line, you start to doubt everything that you believed in because—

JOSH: Are you having a midlife crisis?

ISAAC: Maybe I am. Fuck. Do you think I'm having a midlife crisis?

JOSH: I was joking.

ISAAC: Oh.

(Beat)

ISAAC: How are your folks?

JOSH: They're good.

ISAAC: Good.

(And, a jump-cut:)

EMMA: The point is not that I don't meet men, the point is, I don't have to sit in bars with someone I don't even like. I have people to call if I need to get laid.

AMY: Yes, but they're all twelve.

EMMA: They are not twelve. Some of them are thirty. Some of them are twenty-seven, but some of them are thirty.

AMY: Exactly. How are you going to get married if you're hanging out with thirty year-old men? Or twenty-seven year-old men? They've just learned to tell time.

EMMA: They're lovely.

AMY: I'm sure they are.

EMMA: And they adore me.

AMY: I'm sure they do.

EMMA: Besides, they have no intention of owning me.
They do not compromise my freedom. They allow
me to work incessantly.

AMY: And that is exactly my point!

EMMA: Yes! As it is mine!

aria # 3:
nighmare claire
(or, amsterdam is a cliché)

JOSH: My ex-girlfriend. Claire. She lives in Amsterdam,
and I'm not supposed to know that. Know how I know
it? I read her email. I broke into her account. Which
I know was really bad and like, ethically fucked up,
I know—It's her own fault because she uses all the
same passwords for everything and doesn't change
them. She like, she just uses the same—it's her middle
name—anyway. So I pirated my way into Claire's
hotmail account one day, and there was this e-mail
from her best friend—it was all, "Oh my God that's
so cool that you're in Amsterdam with—" and then,
the whole story. The other guy. The whole story. That's
why you're not supposed to do shit like that. There's
some kind of like, karmic penalty, like you get what
you deserve. Like you find out she's in some strange
place with some really strange dude with money and
dreadlocks. Sometimes, you are just not supposed
to know what you're not supposed to know. I mean,
Amsterdam? It's such a fucking cliché.

scene:
the only single person

EMMA: Can I ask you something?

AMY: Sure.

EMMA: Why didn't you invite me for the Fourth? You had people up here. It sounds like you did— Isaac mentioned—

AMY: You were working. Weren't you working?

EMMA: Actually, I wasn't. You never asked.

AMY: Oh. I just assumed...

EMMA: Is it because I'd have been the only single person?

AMY: It's because I thought you were working.

EMMA: Lately, you don't invite me to things where the only guests are couples.

AMY: Is that true?

EMMA: It is.

AMY: I didn't realize.

EMMA: I want to be invited to things.

AMY: You're here now.

EMMA: But not when it's Couples.

AMY: I didn't realize.

EMMA: I never said anything.

AMY: Well. I'm glad that you're saying something now.

EMMA: And it'll get worse now that you're getting married. You'll only do things with Married People. And then, oh Jesus, you'll do it with Families. Baby people.

AMY: I'm sorry. I honestly didn't realize.

EMMA: I don't want it to be like that.

AMY: It won't be.

EMMA: I want to be included.

AMY: You will be.

EMMA: Promise?

AMY: Sure.

EMMA: Because I want to see you more.

AMY: You're always working.

EMMA: Not always.

AMY: You work as much as Isaac.

EMMA: Well. It's what I do.

AMY: But that's all I'm saying. We don't see each other that much because you're busy. So I have befriended other women.

EMMA: Couples

AMY: Okay. Couples.

EMMA: And I don't see you. And I want to be close like we used to be.

AMY: Emma!

(Meanwhile, back in the attic)

a box like pandora's

JOSH: Hey, Isaac? I know you're just wigging out about the wedding and all, but I mean, I just want to say—

ISAAC: Yes?

JOSH: Think of infinity.

ISAAC: I don't understand.

JOSH: It's what I do lately when I can't—you know, when I'm completely in my head and wigging out. I think of infinity. I imagine it, you know, I see it— like a long red line stretched out in front of me. And that always helps.

ISAAC: Um. Thanks. Josh.

JOSH: It's part of you. That line. And I know you're like in this thing where you're doubting all these choices and whatever, but—think of infinity stretching out in front of you, and then, come back. *(Discovering an old box or trunk...half open...)* Check this out!

ISAAC: Check what out?

(ISAAC and JOSH examine the box. ISAAC opens it. Full of journals and clippings and paraphernalia.)

JOSH: Amy's gonna flip.

the wedding duet

(Both women, to the audience:)

AMY: The key to planning a wedding is to never utter the word "Wedding" to a vendor.

EMMA: I hang out with men in their twenties.

AMY: Vendors hear "Wedding" and they see dollar signs. Anything that is earmarked "Wedding" is immediately jacked up in price so that they can charge you the maximum possible because it's for "Your Special Day".

EMMA: I drink. Not excessively. But some. I do not drink Cosmopolitans.

AMY: Special Day means Financial Ruin. Special Day means bad, sentimental decision-making. Special Day means they want you to go into debt.

EMMA: I travel alone. With my camera, an extra pair of panties and lipstick. I carry my own stash of condoms. Flavored.

AMY: And that will not be happening here.

EMMA: I have become the person I wanted to become.

AMY: Tell all your vendors "family reunion", gathering, anniversary, even—anything but "wedding". You can dash off and do the ceremony behind closed doors and the caterers will never know.

EMMA: But I have become her by myself. And now, I wonder, who will partner me?

AMY: It's the same with the cake. Buy a bakery cake— custom—but don't say "wedding". Later, at home, you can stick those horrible plastic people on top.

EMMA: My peers are mostly married. Men in other relationships come to me because they think I have freedom. I represent something to them, some life they could have had if they hadn't married their college girlfriends. Or their assistants.

AMY: Another thing. People talk to brides like we're mindless virgins. I am not mindless. Or a virgin.

EMMA: I don't believe in Internet Dating. I don't believe in fix-ups (That just sounds like Drive-By, doesn't it?). But I do believe in Love. And whoever he is, he can find me. I am not hard to find.

AMY: The bridal magazines and websites are full of: cake trends, figure fixers, guest books, color combos, to veil or not to veil. And everyone says:

EMMA: Sometimes I think The Loneliness will kill me.

AMY: "This will be the most important day of your life"

EMMA: But it always passes.

AMY: And I think, really?

EMMA: And I am always okay.

AMY: I mean, the most important day of my whole entire life?

scene:
dinner with josh

EMMA: Amy said you just graduated from Purchase?

JOSH: Bard.

EMMA: Right.

JOSH: I took a year off. I mean, before starting. I just finished but I took a year off before starting.

EMMA: Oh?

JOSH: I'm living with my parents til I find something. A job, I mean. Jobs are—not easy to come by.

EMMA: I imagine.

JOSH: Yeah. It pretty much bites all around. Did you guys get out of school and just—have jobs?

AMY: I always had a job.

JOSH: It's not like that anymore. We graduate and are thrown to wolves. You know? No, that's a joke. But seriously, we get out of school and it's like, now what? We just hope to not go to war. Or we do go to war. And then, we hope to survive.

ISAAC: Do you know anyone? Who's gone to...?

JOSH: No. Not really. No.

EMMA: We just worked in coffee shops.

JOSH: We still do that.

ISAAC: (Making fun of himself) Emma and I were "artists".

AMY: I had a real job.

EMMA: Eventually everyone finds their way. *(To* ISAAC, *defending)* And I'm still an artist.

AMY: I always had a real job. I always did.

EMMA: The practical one.

JOSH: I'm waiting. But I don't know what for.

EMMA: I know exactly what you mean.

JOSH: Do you and Isaac work together?

ISAAC: We shared a darkroom once.

EMMA: When people had darkrooms.

JOSH: Now it's all digital.

ISAAC: Emma and I do different kinds of work. *(Teasing)* She's still "An Artist".

EMMA: I photograph weddings.

ISAAC: Not just weddings. Other things.

EMMA: Garbage.

JOSH: No, I bet it's good.

EMMA: No. I mean, I do. I'm obsessed with the things people throw out. As a form of cultural anthropology. Like, the aesthetics of the discarded. So literally. I photograph garbage.

JOSH: Oh.

AMY: Her work's beautiful. The weddings. And the garbage.

EMMA: The weddings are for money. You can make a living on weddings. The garbage however...

JOSH: Wow. You really photograph garbage. That's so...

EMMA: You can learn a lot by what people throw out. Garbage nights in the City are wild—people put all the things they don't want out on the street for other people to take. Oh my God, the week the N Y U dorms

vacate—
these kids leave everything they've accumulated, that
their parents bought for them, right outside. It's insane.

JOSH: Yeah. I had a girlfriend at N Y U. She was insane.
(Beat) Right. So, it's like freecycle.

(They all look confused—)

JOSH: It's a website. It does what you're saying. People
post things online about what they want to
get rid of, and other people, like, answer. But there's
no money allowed, so it all has to be, you know,
totally free. People are like "Hey, I'm looking for
a space heater," or like, "I have a bunch of packing
tape—anyone want it?" and then people meet up and
exchange their stuff.

EMMA: Wow.

ISAAC: Oh brave new world....

JOSH: Well, like, it's how, you know, how the Internet
might be able to create *actual* community or, like,
alternative models of commerce. I mean, theoretically,
we could all be doing things really differently, you
know?

EMMA: What did you study? At Bard?

JOSH: Psychology. But I'm not going to do anything
with the degree. I'm actually thinking more about...
I don't know. Psych was so that I could understand
people, but I don't think that's really what I want to
do with my life. My whole life. I look at the world
right now, and okay, okay, we need psychologists,
we do—but I think we might need a lot of things.
I don't know, right now I just work in a coffee shop—
and here, for Isaac—til I can get enough money
together to move on. Figure it out. Move on.

AMY: Are you dying to get to the City?

JOSH: No. I like it up here. I don't know if New York is for me. New York depresses the fuck out of me actually. It just does. Bums me out. It's so expensive, and there's no parking. And everyone's so (*He makes a face to indicate faux-sophistication*) I don't want to stay at my parents or anything. But I wouldn't mind moving to some smaller city. Like Northampton. Or Brattleboro. I hear Minneapolis is cool. There are really good bands there. And it's like a city, but it's not like New York. I'd love to find a city that is a city but not The City. You know what I mean?

EMMA: No. I always just wanted New York.

AMY: When we were twenty-two, it was the land of our dreams.

EMMA: It still is. For me.

AMY: But when we were twenty-two—

EMMA: When we lived together.

AMY: And stayed out all night—

ISAAC: Before me.

AMY: After you, too.

EMMA: We had—

AMY: All sorts of—

(*The girls giggle, and for a moment, you can see who they were together, at twenty-two, staying out all night. ISAAC opens another bottle of wine.*)

ISAAC: Okay, who wants more?

(*They all raise their hands as if they're in grade school. ISAAC refills all of their glasses.*)

JOSH: And now, these guys are buying a house and getting married. That must make you feel—

ISAAC: We didn't buy the house, we inherited it.

JOSH: Same diff.

AMY: Not the same diff, Sweetie. Financially, it's a totally different "diff".

EMMA: To you, we must all seem—

JOSH: You guys are great. You know, there's this thing in our culture, where people don't hang out with people who aren't the same generation or whatever, but emotional intelligence kinda defies its chronological deal, and you guys are like that. Like, you fall into this rad void between the generations, and we can all relate. Do you know what I mean?

ISAAC: Thanks, I think?

EMMA: I know what you mean.

ISAAC: Emma specializes in the rad void.

AMY: Honey.

ISAAC: What? She does. (To EMMA, *just a little drunk*) Don't you? You do. The guys? (To JOSH) She has this thing for Rad Void. (To EMMA) Who's the guy right now?

EMMA: No one.

ISAAC: That's not what I heard.

(EMMA *shoots* AMY *a look.*)

AMY: I may have mentioned something. Unintentionally. Casually. In passing.

EMMA: He's a friend.

AMY: But he's twelve, and he has a girlfriend.

EMMA: We're friends.

AMY: They're having an emotional affair.

JOSH: What's an emotional affair?

AMY: They talk about books, take walks, hold hands, write letters. Everything except sex. I'm glad you didn't bring him, Em.

ISAAC: Bring him *here*?

AMY: She wanted to bring him here.

EMMA: We don't hold hands.

AMY: They're having the College Relationship.

ISAAC: I had sex in college.

AMY: I did too.

JOSH: Yeah. Me too.

EMMA: Sure. Me too. Sometimes. Maybe. Look. He's a companion.

AMY: But he has a girlfriend.

ISAAC: It sounds like a friendship. She says it's a friendship.

AMY: *(To* EMMA*)* But you're pretending. *(To the others)* She's pretending.

EMMA: What am I pretending?

AMY: That you're having a relationship.

EMMA: We are having a relationship.

AMY: But don't you want more?

ISAAC: Why can't they just be friends?

AMY: He's totally cheating on his girlfriend.

EMMA: We've never touched.

AMY: But it's an emotional affair. You're pretending—

EMMA: We're having the relationship in Jane Austen novels.

ISAAC: The kind where you entertain one another's intellects?

EMMA: I'd say, "stimulate" rather than "entertain".

ISAAC: Would you?

JOSH: Get back to this pretending thing. What's she pretending?

AMY: Emotional affairs count.

EMMA: Since when?

AMY: Since always.

ISAAC: Define an "emotional affair".

JOSH: Please.

EMMA: Oh my God.

AMY: It's an affair in your heart. No one crosses the line, so everyone can say, later, that they were faithful. But something happens. You can feel it. The air changes. And everyone knows, but no one admits. I know about these things.

ISAAC: Because you've had them? You've had emotional affairs?

AMY: No. Just because I know about these things. You can feel the difference. A line is crossed.

EMMA: I disagree! There are many kinds of relationships that people can have without being transgressive. There are all sorts of permutations—

JOSH: I think Amy's right. I mean, there's this girl I'm friends with, like from school, and she, I mean, nothing's ever happened, but I kinda keep the whole thing separate, you know, like hip-pocketed, in case it does. You know what I mean? Like I *never* talk to her about other girls. I want to keep her like, an option. Is that what you mean?

ISAAC: Listen. Emma. It's time for something real. You need a Guy. A Guy who wears Guy Socks. And has a Guy Job. And a Guy Haircut. And he should be our age. And no girlfriend. Someone who is ready to be a part of your life. Who shows up, ready. Who moves toward you without ambivalence or ambiguity.

EMMA: Oh right. Like that happens.

ISAAC: It's time you stopped avoiding this.

EMMA: I'm not avoiding it.

AMY: I'm telling you. Sit in bars with Wendy.

ISAAC: Don't sit in bars with Wendy. Wendy's awful.

EMMA: See? Besides, who are these guys Wendy's meeting? I want An Equal.

ISAAC: Equal to you or equal to Wendy?

EMMA: Equal to me.

ISAAC: That might be hard.

EMMA: Certainly in bars. Besides, I'm not looking to meet anyone. I don't believe it happens that way.

JOSH: What happens what way?

EMMA: What I want.

ISAAC: What do you want?

AMY: She wants something that doesn't exist.

EMMA: I want something that hasn't been invented yet. Or remembered. Maybe it was invented a long time ago and we forgot and need to remember it. A love between equals. In which each person is free to become his or her best self. That is what I am looking for.

ISAAC: That sounds unrealistic. Can't you just have something real?

EMMA: Of course! But that is not what—

AMY: —"what's happening".

ISAAC: So what are you going to do?

EMMA: I am not going *to do* anything! *(And then, getting more defensive than she'd like)* We all need to stop discussing my being single like it's a disease. There is nothing wrong with my life. I like my life. I have a good life. With all sorts of stimulating and complicated if non-traditional relationships! Both including sex and not including sex. Lets all change the subject now. Please.

(Awkward pause)

JOSH: Yeah. Well, I should go home. Thanks for dinner. It was great. *(To* EMMA*)* Um, nice meeting you—

ISAAC: Thanks for helping out today.

JOSH: No problem. It was cool. That box, Man—Amy, we found this box full of—you're gonna flip when you see—

ISAAC: Coral's things.

JOSH: Programs, diaries, clippings—

ISAAC: I'll show you.

AMY: I can't wait. *(To* JOSH*)* Josh, will you take food home? Dessert? Take some dessert.

*(*AMY *leads* JOSH *back to the kitchen, leaving* EMMA *and* ISAAC *alone.)*

ISAAC: You okay?

*(*EMMA *shrugs.)*

ISAAC: Come on.

*(*EMMA *and* ISAAC *take a bottle of wine and head outside.)*

(As EMMA *and* ISAAC *leave, or shortly thereafter,* AMY *re-enters the room. She heads for the boxes and starts to rummage through them.)*

(While the following exchange between ISAAC *and* EMMA *takes place,* AMY *is going through these boxes.)*

(Meanwhile, EMMA *and* ISAAC *sit outside, looking at the stars.)*

ISAAC: Coral was forty when she married my dad.

*(*EMMA *nods.)*

ISAAC: And she did not have kids. Of her own. Before us.

EMMA: She told me that. She told me, that morning, she said—

ISAAC: "The thing you want wants you back?"

EMMA: That she had no regrets.

(Meanwhile, AMY *opens Coral's box. It's full of fabulous, distinctive objects: opera glasses, a great vintage hat, scrapbooks, sketchbooks, journals.)*

*(*AMY *opens a worn journal and begins to read.*

ISAAC: I shouldn't have said anything. About you. And the guys.

*(*AMY *reads:)*

AMY: "April, 1998. Isaac is here, visiting. He and Amy are planning to move in together. He's here now."

ISAAC: She reorganized my desk.

EMMA: I'm sorry.

AMY: "I sent him out—so that I could spend the rest of the morning talking to her."

ISAAC: I've told her, I've said, I really like things the way they are. But she—

EMMA: Always has a better idea. Of how things should be.

AMY: "...She reminds me of myself at her age. I see so much inside of her, how complicated she is, how much she wants. She's engaged in some kind of passionate argument with the most basic facts about her life and because of this, I think she could be a remarkable partner for him."

(ISAAC *laughs*.)

ISAAC: She had everything color-coded. Little hanging files everywhere, it was— *(Awful)*

EMMA: It was probably remarkable.

AMY: "Amy is sweet—"

EMMA: Efficient, organized, spatially intelligent.

AMY: "...but Emma is special."

ISAAC: And now I can't find anything.

AMY: "It is love, but they don't know it. I watch them and it's so obvious to me, this thing that both are completely unaware of. I wish I could say..."

EMMA: She thinks I need a man.

AMY: "You are with the wrong person"

ISAAC: You don't need anything.

AMY: "I wish I could tell them: this is what love is."

ISAAC: I think you're perfect—

AMY: "Someone you don't have to change. Who already appreciates exactly who you are and who can match that. "I wish you could see this in one another."

ISAAC: Exactly the way you are.

(AMY *closes the journal. Goes upstairs*)

scene:
questions

(ISAAC *comes to bed.* AMY *is up, waiting.*)

AMY: I have questions.

ISAAC: Shoot.

AMY: I know you would never lie to me.

ISAAC: True.

AMY: So, tell me about the weekend you spent with Emma.

ISAAC: What do you mean?

AMY: Did you bring Emma to this house?

ISAAC: I don't know what you mean.

AMY: Did you and Emma come up to the house without me? And maybe you just forgot to say something because—because that's how you are and not because you had anything to hide?

ISAAC: I still don't understand the question.

AMY: Did you and Em come up here alone, without me? I think that's an easy question. Which word do you not understand?

ISAAC: Did she say we did?

AMY: Did you?

ISAAC: Well. Once. Yes. Yes, we did. Once.

AMY: And you never mentioned it?

ISAAC: It wasn't—I don't know.

AMY: Where was I?

ISAAC: Out of town.

AMY: Why did you bring Emma to this house?

ISAAC: It was a long time ago.

AMY: Like April 5, 1998?

ISAAC: I guess.

AMY: What happened? When you brought her here?

ISAAC: Nothing happened.

AMY: But you never mentioned it.

ISAAC: I guess not. It wasn't—Amy, it wasn't a conspiracy or anything. We just—

AMY: Didn't tell me.

ISAAC: What do you want me to say?

AMY: I want you to tell me what happened the night you and my best friend came up to the house without me?

ISAAC: I'm not playing this game.

AMY: I'm not playing it either. I am asking you a direct question.

ISAAC: What does she say happened?

AMY: I haven't spoken to her. I'm asking you.

ISAAC: If you haven't spoken to her—I don't—I don't understand and I don't see why you won't just ask me what you want to ask me.

(AMY *holds up a worn leather book.*)

AMY: Your stepmother kept a journal. Did you know that? It's amazing. It says all sorts of amazing things. She had a lot of opinions.

ISAAC: Coral kept a— Can you tell me exactly what—?

AMY: It says that you and Emma are in love.

scene:
the first awake

(*Day 2*)

(EMMA *in the kitchen alone, just the same as at the start of the play.* ISAAC *enters. Also the same, only different.*)

EMMA: We are always the first awake. Any time you and I are in the same house, I know that I will see you, before anyone else, first thing in the morning. Other people love to sleep late, Amy loves to sleep late, but you and me, we're alike, we—

ISAAC: We should talk.

EMMA: Amy sleeps late. But—

ISAAC: We should really talk.

EMMA: This sounds ominous.

ISAAC: Not ominous. Misguided.

(AMY *enters—*)

EMMA: Ame, there's coffee. And it's strong.

AMY: You tell her?

EMMA: Tell me what?

ISAAC: I was just about to.

AMY: I'll be upstairs. Reading. *(She leaves.)*

EMMA: Is she okay?

ISAAC: Amy found a box of things that belonged to Coral. In the attic. And there was, Coral kept, there was this "diary" *(This should sound like a dirty word.)* She—about the night we were here.

EMMA: Oh.

ISAAC: Yes. Coral had a lot to say about us. Aapparently, we made her remember my father and apparently, also, Coral believed—that you and I— were in love. Or should be in love. Or were meant to fall in love. Only we didn't know it.

EMMA: *(Alarmed)* That's ridiculous.

ISAAC: Yes. And even worse, the really beautiful part is, Amy believes her.

EMMA: Amy believes her?

ISAAC: Amy believes her.

scene:
selective, elective, honesty

(AMY *sits, reading the journal, engrossed.*)

AMY: "They move together like elegant machinery.
She challenges him in ways that Amy—"

(EMMA *enters, overlapping with the above.*)

EMMA: Amy?

AMY: I can't talk to you yet. I'll let you know when
I can talk to you.

EMMA: But, Amy—

AMY: Yes?

EMMA: You don't seriously think—

AMY: What?

EMMA: Well. Anything. You don't seriously think
anything. Do you?

AMY: I don't know what I think. Why did you come
here and never tell me about it?

EMMA: I don't know.

AMY: I don't know what to think.

EMMA: Amy, nothing happened. We came up here
once, but it wasn't//illicit or—

AMY: Illicit?

EMMA: //anything. He and I are friends. Like you and
I are friends. We came up to get away. We were
talking, working late, in the darkroom—

AMY: He and you are not friends like you and I. You
and I are different.

EMMA: We drove up and crashed and in the morning
I shot some pictures and then, we left. Nothing ever

happened, and I don't know why we never told you—
but—

AMY: We were friends first.

EMMA: It was all completely harmless.

AMY: And *we're* both women.

EMMA: What does that mean? We're all friends. Am
I supposed to not be friends with Isaac because he's
your boyfriend?

AMY: Partner.

EMMA: Sure. Does that mean I can't—also—?

AMY: It means your primary loyalty is to me.

EMMA: I don't think about things that way.

AMY: Do you love him?

EMMA: Like I love you.

AMY: Are you lying?

EMMA: I don't lie.

AMY: You've dated married men.

EMMA: That's not fair. Once.

AMY: Twice.

EMMA: The second was a mistake.

AMY: They were both mistakes. The point is that you
do lie.

EMMA: No, Amy, I don't—this is—

AMY: This is honesty? It's selective?

EMMA: It's not elective.

AMY: I didn't say "elective", I said "selective" —you
select what to—

EMMA: It was a long time ago. And it was platonic. We
are friends. We are all three friends with one another.

Who knows what Coral thinks she saw. Who knows?
Amy.

AMY: Please don't keep saying my name.

EMMA: What will help? What can I do?

AMY: Nothing. You can't do anything.

EMMA: I'm sorry we didn't tell you about that night.
It was so long ago, but it really wasn't—

AMY: —illicit.

EMMA: Yes! We never said, no one ever said "Don't tell
Amy" —it just didn't come up. We never said don't tell
Amy.

AMY: But you didn't. You didn't tell Amy. Which
means, that something *did* happen. Even if nothing
happened, something happened, or you would have
talked about it. Ten years! And you could have. There
were so many times when you could have. There was
some reason that you wanted to keep this from me,
something that wasn't right, otherwise, you'd have
talked about it!

EMMA: But—does everything have to be—? What if we
didn't need to? What if I didn't want to? What if I *liked*
how we all trust each other enough that I wouldn't
need to— Do you know what I mean?

AMY: No! I don't! I don't have secrets!

EMMA: But it's not about you! *(Beat?)* That doesn't
sound right. I don't mean it's not about you, I just
mean—

AMY: You mean that there's some piece of you that
has to have something behind my back. You mean
that you've been holding onto some kind of special
relationship with my fiance for—

EMMA: That is not true!

(Beat)

AMY: I don't trust you.

EMMA: You don't trust me? We've been friends for twenty years.

AMY: And I just realized that I do not trust you. I see the way you look at him.

EMMA: How do I look at him?

AMY: Like he's Superman. You look at Isaac like he is—

EMMA: I don't—

AMY: You've always done that. It's because you didn't have a father. At least that's how I always—

EMMA: It's because what?

AMY: Because you didn't have a father. You're awestruck by men. There are studies.

EMMA: What???

AMY: What were you doing in this house, and why does Coral have journal entries about elegant machinery?

EMMA: I don't even know what that means.

AMY: She says you fit together like elegant machinery.

EMMA: She was Swiss!

AMY: This is serious. What were you doing together in this house without me? And why didn't you say anything?

EMMA: I don't know. I don't know why. It's just— I guess whatever that night was, it just—wanted to stay between us. Not because anything happened, just because, I don't know why. And the longer I didn't say anything, I guess the more it seemed like a *thing*, but it wasn't. It wasn't.

AMY: Why are you still alone? Who are you waiting for?

EMMA: I don't know what you mean.

AMY: Don't you? I've had to listen to you—and all of your stories and all of these—men who break your heart—all these years. And I've never said anything, I've never said anything. You come to Isaac and me to get taken care of. And we pay attention to you, we listen, we take care of your poor disabled ill equipped free falling broken heart—and you get all the attention because you're the special one, and I don't trust you. I don't care what happened. In this house. I care—what I care about—is that you were here—and the two of you kept a secret from me. Can't anything just be mine!?

EMMA: Can I read it? Can I at least—?

AMY: No.

(AMY *holds the journal close.* EMMA *moves towards her and* AMY *moves away, holding the journal to her body.*)

EMMA: How can you not trust me?

AMY: You flirt.

EMMA: What!?

AMY: With both of us. You always have. These twenty-five year-olds you date, they may let you boss them around, but they wise up, you know. No one thinks—Josh doesn't think—that it's any great mark of your maturity or evolution that you can't set realistic boundaries or expectations and have realistic relationships.

EMMA: You're really angry right now, and I'm going to—

AMY: I want you to leave.

(AMY *leaves the room, taking the journal with her.*
EMMA *is stunned.*)

scene:
a diary is subjective.

(Mid-fight)

ISAAC: But it's is a wholly subjective account. This is not an objective record of the weekend.

AMY: So now it's a weekend? I thought it was one night.

ISAAC: My point is that this is someone's opinion. This is not factual. This is subjective.

AMY: Do you wish you were with her?

ISAAC: This is crazy. Amy, nothing happened.

AMY: You keep saying that like it means something. And it doesn't mean anything. It doesn't. I don't care whether something happened. That's not what I care about.

ISAAC: So what do you care about?

AMY: I care that she wrote it. I care that you never told me you were up here with my friend.

ISAAC: Our friend

AMY: No. She was my friend. She was my friend first. And I care that there was something, something Coral saw, something that made her write that—I care that something I believed is different than how I believed it. I care that there's a "story" now and that—everything is—to be questioned.

ISAAC: What's "to be questioned"?

AMY: Everything. All of it.

ISAAC: Just because she wrote it doesn't mean it's true. Coral had an active imagination. She missed my father, I don't know. There are many reasons she could have written whatever she wrote. A journal is not objective. And people project. People project all the time. Maybe she was talking about herself.

AMY: She was in love with you too?

ISAAC: Emma isn't in love with me.

AMY: How do you know?

ISAAC: How do I know what!?

AMY: How do you know anything!? You don't even know what you feel half the time. I have to tell you.

ISAAC: That's bullshit. I let you tell me because it's easier than— Listen. I know because I know. Some things are objective. There is factual information available.

AMY: What is the factual information?

ISAAC: The factual information: I brought Emma to the house. We shot pictures. We slept in separate beds, in separate rooms. She had breakfast with Coral. We shot more pictures. We drove back to New York. That is the information. That is all of the information. That is the entire record of what happened in April of 1998. When you were out of town.

AMY: Good. Thank you. I have to go now.

ISAAC: Where are you going?

AMY: Over to Josh's. Josh's parents.

ISAAC: What!?

AMY: You're sweet, but he's special. *(She leaves.)*

scene:
more than one kind of everything

(Citronella candles and moonlight. AMY *and* JOSH *sit, outside.)*

AMY: When I met Isaac's family, first at a dinner in the City, later up here, when I met his dad and Coral, I thought, "These are real New Yorkers." These people are educated, cultured, they read *The New York Times* and not just on Sundays. They attend lectures and concerts. These children had music lessons and everyone went to good schools in the East and engaged in political debate over meals and listened to public radio. It was different than anything I'd known. My parents were cheap. I'm frugal, but my parents were cheap. But Isaac's parents were the opposite. They had more than one kind of everything in the house. In the refrigerator. More than one kind of juice. More than one kind of milk—regular for Isaac's dad, skim for Coral, rice milk for his sister Maria— More than one kind of coat—day coat, evening coat, bad weather coat. And so on. It amazed me. This was the life I moved here for. This is what I wanted. More than one kind. Of everything.

JOSH: You have that.

AMY: Yes. I do. *(Beat)* Listen to this: *(She opens the journal and reads.)* "Protection against heartbreak will not save you. Only heartbreak itself can save you."

JOSH: I thought you were happy.

AMY: We are.

JOSH: So what's the problem?

AMY: There are so many.

JOSH: Like?

AMY: Well, like his dead stepmother thought he was in love with my best friend. That's one.

JOSH: That's rough.

AMY: Yeah. But there are others. If there weren't other problems, other reasons, this wouldn't be so upsetting.

JOSH: Relationships are hard, Man.

AMY: They sure are, Man.

(AMY *and* JOSH *eat cookies, swing their legs from the dock. They burn those candles that fight off bugs. Citronella)*

AMY: Do you have a girlfriend?

JOSH: Not really. Not right now. I did. But not right now.

AMY: How come?

JOSH: I don't know. My girlfriend was—she was—and I don't want to do that again. And girls, you know, they say they're just having sex, but they're not. They want things—other things, unspoken things. And after awhile, it's just boring.

AMY: It sure is.

JOSH: Plus, I like high maintenance women.

AMY: You're twenty-three. Who's "high maintenance"?

JOSH: You'd be surprised.

(AMY *and* JOSH *laugh.)*

JOSH: But it's more than that too. I'm not good—I'm not good to them. They're high maintenance and all—but I—I like how they keep me off balance. I don't like it when it's easy. So I kind of set them up to be crazy, and then they are—crazy—and then I get to say, "Well, she's crazy" and then I don't have to really be there— you know, with them. Because really, I'm not entirely sure what it's all for.

AMY: Yeah.

JOSH: Hey, Amy?

AMY: Yes?

JOSH: Do you, um—

AMY: Yes?

JOSH: Do you want to be with Isaac? I mean, do you want to marry him?

(AMY *says nothing.*)

JOSH: Because it's just this sense I get. I don't think you really care about all this diary shit. I just think you're looking for an Out. And that's okay. It's totally okay. You can have an Out. If that's what you want. *(Beat)* Is it okay? That I said that?

AMY: It's okay. *(She takes a deep breath, then, trying to explain.)* We make commitments when we get older. We make promises.

JOSH: Sure, but I just think, like commitment isn't about—I mean, if you get on a bus and like, you think it's headed for New York City but then you realize the bus is actually going upstate to like, Albany, you know, you wouldn't stay on the bus. You'd get off the bus and try to get on the one going to where you're going. Right? So, I think it should be like that. You commit and Man, you try, you know, you stay faithful to it and all—but if it starts going to Albany—you can't go to Albany, it's fucking awful there.

AMY: But it's a lot to ask.

JOSH: Albany?

AMY: Leaving.

JOSH: I guess. *(Beat)* But what else do you want to do? Stay?

(Beat)

AMY: I don't know.

(Beat)

AMY: Do you really get that sense?

(Beat. JOSH doesn't answer.))

AMY: I should go back.

(But AMY doesn't. They sit a moment longer. Something in her, releases, softens.)

AMY: Thank you.

JOSH: What for?

AMY: Listening.

JOSH: Oh. No problem. I like listening. I majored in Psych, remember?

(AMY laughs. JOSH starts to take her back to the house.)

JOSH: Can I um, do you want, can I hug you?

(Beat. And awkwardly, but sweetly, they do.)

AMY: Hey, Josh? If I leave Isaac, you want to have a baby with me?

(JOSH looks terrified.)

JOSH: Um—

AMY: I'm joking.

JOSH: Oh.

(JOSH still looks terrified.)

AMY: Sweetie, I'm really joking.

(AMY kisses JOSH's cheek and walks ahead.)

JOSH: Okay. Yeah.

scene:
what if it were true?

EMMA: I keep trying to remember.

ISAAC: What?

EMMA: All of it. What we did. What I was thinking. What we talked about. How it all felt. I remember driving up here, it was late, I needed to get away that night, it was a relief to have somewhere to go. And you said, in the car, you said, "It is no longer viable to be with someone who can't receive you"—

ISAAC: It was true. It's still true.

EMMA: I was getting over—

ISAAC: The One Who Didn't Talk.

EMMA: But it is ten years later, and I have still not been received.

ISAAC: You don't do so bad.

EMMA: Nothing happened.

ISAAC: Of course it didn't.

EMMA: We were not in love.

ISAAC: But this other person said—

EMMA: That we were.

ISAAC: And now it's like we're supposed to feel guilty for something that—

EMMA: Never happened.

ISAAC: It's crazy.

EMMA: It is.

ISAAC: We were never even—

EMMA: You would never even have looked at me.

ISAAC: What does that mean?

EMMA: When we were twenty-five. I wasn't exactly in your league.

ISAAC: You were lovely.

EMMA: No. I'm lovely now. But not at twenty-five.

ISAAC: You were. Not that I—

EMMA: Of course.

ISAAC: Nothing happened.

EMMA: I know. *(Beat)* But what if, and I'm just saying, what if...?

ISAAC: What if she's right?

EMMA: What if we were, and we didn't know?

ISAAC: I don't know. She wasn't right. I mean, not that I don't find you—because I do—but—she wasn't right. *(Beat)* And even if I did, I couldn't—because that would be—and I'd never—even if for one small moment, I wanted to—

EMMA: It's not even an emotional affair.

ISAAC: Well.

EMMA: Is it?

ISAAC: I don't know.

EMMA: Oh.

ISAAC: I don't know.

EMMA: Oh.

ISAAC: I mean—I don't know.

EMMA: Oh.

(Beat. It gets more dangerous. EMMA and ISAAC are standing at the edge of a very tall cliff.)

ISAAC: Who would we be?

EMMA: If we were lovers?

(ISAAC *nods. Then a long pause in which neither can answer the question. As if the question itself will send them falling down the aforementioned cliff*)

EMMA: I don't know.

ISAAC: It all sort of just happened. To us. I met her, I met you, you two were always together— But if I had the presence of mind, if I'd noticed you, if it were you—?

EMMA: But you didn't. And it wasn't. And I don't know.

ISAAC: You're right. Of course you are. But—if we had—under very different circumstances—

(EMMA *and* ISAAC *decide not to fall.*)

EMMA: I think we'd be like we are.

ISAAC: Good. Good. Friends.

EMMA: Yes.

(EMMA *and* ISAAC *are in agreement. But something starts to happen nonetheless. They go to hug one another, and it's platonic—only, it lasts a long time. Just a little too long for platonic.*)

(EMMA *and* ISAAC *find one another's mouths and they almost kiss, or start to—whatever it is, it's hot and forbidden, full of a question that never got asked—until she pulls away without having kissed him.*)

EMMA: I can't.

(*Beat.* EMMA *and* ISAAC *turn away from one another, and she leaves the room.*)

scene:
letting go

(The next morning)

ISAAC: So that's it?

AMY: Just about.

ISAAC: It can't be—just—don't you want to try to—

AMY: I don't want to—anything.

ISAAC: But—

AMY: I feel better than I have in a really long time. I've been working so hard to get this thing, not one thing, but an entire group of things. I've been trying and working— and suddenly, suddenly, when I imagine not having to keep you—to keep you moving—to keep you active and together and—suddenly I feel remarkably free. I can do whatever I want now. I never have to push you forward again. I don't want to push you forward. I just want to do things very differently.

ISAAC: This makes no sense. You can—whatever you want—with me.

AMY: No. We worked enough. It's time for something else.

ISAAC: I don't understand.

AMY: I'm not suggesting that our relationships are over. Any of them. I'm just suggesting—maybe a great many things we thought were true are not.

ISAAC: Don't do this.

AMY: No. It's good. What I'm doing is very good. You just don't know it yet. *(She smiles.)*

scene:
our greatest hits

(AMY *and* EMMA, *sitting outside*)

AMY: Sullivan Street.

EMMA: Our first apartment. No bathtub.

AMY: Fourth floor walk-up. It was so small.

EMMA: Do you remember how I took baths at other people's places?

AMY: We had a stall shower.

EMMA: I love baths.

AMY: You took them at that neighbor's place.

EMMA: The Canadian girl.

AMY: She was sweet. Whatever happened to her?

EMMA: I don't know. She let me take baths.

AMY: Exactly. That was sweet.

EMMA: Do you remember how we used to wake up every Sunday and go to brunch?

AMY: And how you'd call—you would get on the phone and call all our friends—every week—just to remind them. And we always went to the same place.

EMMA: I liked the coffee there.

AMY: The place where we saw Lou Reed.

EMMA: Just that once.

AMY: Right. But we went there every week.

EMMA: They had the best coffee.

AMY: And seeing Lou Reed wasn't half bad either. We lived in that apartment for five whole years. That's amazing by New York City standards.

EMMA: And you met Isaac.

AMY: And everything changed.

EMMA: Not at first. Not at first it didn't. I remember
when you first brought him home. And how we all
were together, how much fun we had. That first brunch
with Isaac.

AMY: We stayed all day. They were going to get rid
of us but he tipped so well. And we stayed there all
afternoon. We didn't have anything else to do besides
be together. All three of us. We were falling in love,
him and me and me and you and him and us and,
all of us with each other.

EMMA: The three of us were a pair. For a while.

AMY: Hey, remember that guy you were dating? When
Isaac and I first met? The Jamaican?

EMMA: He wasn't Jamaican. And that's not who I was
dating when you and Isaac met. I was dating Paul.
I was starting to date Paul.

AMY: Oh right. I liked the Jamaican.

EMMA: He wasn't Jamaican. He was from New York,
he just talked funny.

AMY: What ever happened to him?

EMMA: I don't know. We lost touch. I think he's in
Santa Fe.

AMY: That's too bad.

EMMA: Santa Fe?

AMY: I liked him.

EMMA: I wanted to live with Paul more than I can
even begin to describe. I wanted him to move into the
apartment on Sullivan Street—we'd install a bathtub—
and just, be together. The problem was, I kept phrasing
it like, "Do you think this is something you want?"

And he kept saying maybe, but sleeping with other women.

AMY: That's why telling is usually better than asking. I am a fan of the ultimatum. At least, I was.

EMMA: I hate all that. It's the behavior our mother's generation broke free of.

AMY: Our mothers did not end up well. Either of them.

EMMA: That's not the point. The point is, Ethics. The point is, how are you going to live your life? The point is—

AMY: The point is— *(She lets go the argument.)* I don't know anymore.

(Beat)

EMMA: I'm sorry.

AMY: I'm not.

EMMA: We weren't in love.

AMY: Him and you? You and me? Him and us? Which of us were not in love?

EMMA: I don't know.

AMY: It doesn't matter. *(Beat)* Josh will take you to the train.

EMMA: Okay.

AMY: They leave every hour.

EMMA: I know.

AMY: I'm not angry. I just have things to do here. Plans to change. Caterers to cancel. I'll call you.

EMMA: Will we be okay?

AMY: You and me?

EMMA: Yes. You and me.

AMY: Will we still be friends?

(EMMA nods.)

AMY: Who knows? I don't really know. *(She smiles. This is genuine—and open—and trusting.)* Lets just not know.

END OF PLAY

CPSIA information can be obtained
at www.ICGtesting.com
Printed in the USA
BVHW040931050121
597029BV00017B/382